T0132210

What Do I See?
ANIMALS IN THE FOREST

Mbenabo Goumbala

AuthorHouse™
1663 Liberty Drive
Bloomington, IN 47403
www.authorhouse.com
Phone: 833-262-8899

Because of the dynamic nature of the Internet, any web addresses or links contained in this book may have changed
since publication and may no longer be valid. The views expressed in this work are solely those of the author and do
not necessarily reflect the views of the publisher, and the publisher hereby disclaims any responsibility for them.

Any people depicted in stock imagery provided by Getty Images are models,
and such images are being used for illustrative purposes only.
Certain stock imagery © Getty Images.

This book is printed on acid-free paper.

ISBN: 979-8-8230-2253-8 (sc)
ISBN: 979-8-8230-2254-5 (e)

Print information available on the last page.

Published by AuthorHouse 02/15/2024

authorHOUSE®

I

see

The Lion

I

see

The snake

I

see

The elephant

I

see

The monkey

I

see

The crocodile

I see

The zebra

I

see

The tiger

I

see

The bear

I see

The Fox

I see

The giraffe

I see

The rabbit

I

see

The deer

I

see

The camel

I

see

The donkey

I

see

The cheetah

I

see

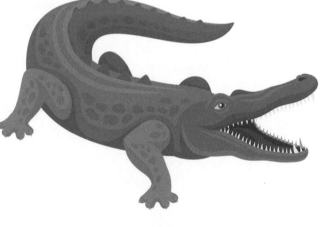

The alligator

I

see

The kangaroo

I see

The buffalo

I

see

The jaguar

I

see

The owl

I

see

The lizard

Printed in the United States
by Baker & Taylor Publisher Services